A LETTER TO THE BOUND

Biblical Truths for a Life of True Freedom

Crystal Boswell

This book is a work of non-fiction. Unless otherwise noted, the author and the publisher make no explicit guarantees as to the accuracy of the information contained in this book and in some cases, names of people and places have been altered to protect their privacy.

WestBow Press books may be ordered through booksellers or by contacting:

WestBow Press
A Division of Thomas Nelson & Zondervan
1663 Liberty Drive
Bloomington, IN 47403
www.westbowpress.com
844-714-3454

Because of the dynamic nature of the Internet, any web addresses or links contained in this book may have changed since publication and may no longer be valid. The views expressed in this work are solely those of the author and do not necessarily reflect the views of the publisher, and the publisher hereby disclaims any responsibility for them.

ISBN: 978-1-6642-8144-8 (sc)
ISBN: 978-1-6642-8146-2 (hc)
ISBN: 978-1-6642-8145-5 (e)

Library of Congress Control Number: 2022919168

Print information available on the last page.

WestBow Press rev. date: 10/20/2022

1

THE TWO PRISONERS

A LETTER TO THE BOUND

In the small, dark, damp cell, there sat two prisoners who had been locked up for quite some time. The men sat on their filthy cots, wearing heavy chains. With no sunlight or fresh air, the cell emitted an aroma of mildew. The first, Tom, had been in this cell for almost thirteen years. Dave had been there so long that he'd forgotten what natural daylight even looked like. The men didn't get any visitors; the atmosphere of the dungeon wasn't exactly appealing. In fact, the only other person in their cold world was the huge prison guard, Damian. Damian was seven feet two and weighed about 350 pounds. The prisoners knew when Damian was on his way to visit them. His loud footsteps were always followed by an evil laugh that tormented the men.

On each of Damian's visits, he teased the guys and reminded them of all their failures. He made sure they knew that they would always be prisoners in this awful place. The men only had distant memories of their loved ones on the outside. Now Damian was all they knew. Damian wasn't all bad, though. From time to time, when the men felt down, Damian had a way of cheering them up. You see, Damian was a mastermind. He ran his own private business, which allowed him to hack into people's bank accounts and steal their information. Through manipulation, Tom and Dave stole people's information for Damian. Afterwards, he left them strange little candies as a reward. Tom and Dave hated doing this for Damian because they knew that they were stealing from people, most of whom happened to be their own family members. But they feared Damian and really loved his strange candy. Stealing became easier for them because of their obsession with the candy. Tom and Dave realized that they were becoming OK with stealing and decided that they needed to break out of this prison.

One afternoon the two men had a visitor. Only this time, it wasn't Damian. No, this visitor was altogether different. When he approached the cell door, the men were afraid. But somehow they knew that this man had come to set them free. He was an answer to their prayers. He looked at with more kindness than Damian did. The visitor offered Tom and Dave salvation. To be set free, they must confess that this man was the only person able to save them from this prison and wholeheartedly believe that he had already paid their bail.

Quickly, they decided that this deal was too good to pass up! Their confession was made, and they believed wholeheartedly. *Snap* went the old chains that had held them bound for so long. As for the prison doors? Well, those too were wide open!

"How can this be?" Tom asked, but Dave was already leaving the cell.

"Come on, man. Let's get outta here!"

Tom began to shake off the remnants of his chains. When they got out of the cell, they were taken to a place that looked like a hospital. Tom and Dave were given a much-needed bath, which caused them to feel renewed. Their baths seemed to wash away all the debris from the cell, allowing them to be truly free of their old lives.

"Wow, man, you look good," they said to each other. Once they were cleaned up, they parted ways and went out to reunite with their families.

Tom was walking down Straight Street when he spotted a familiar face to his left: Damian. Tom got nervous and began to panic as the huge bully came toward him.

"Now, Damian, wait. I-I can explain. You see wh-what had happened was …" Tom stuttered nervously.

"Where did you think you were goin'? How dare you try to escape! You remember all the crimes you committed? You didn't think that you could just get away without finishing your prison time, did you? Who do you think you are?" Damian asked. He grabbed Tom by the throat, put the chains back on him, and threw him into his old cell.

After some time had passed, Dave began to worry about Tom. He went to Tom's family and asked what he'd been up to, saying that he wanted to catch up with him. Tom's family was surprised to see Dave doing so well and looking so good.

"Haven't you heard? Tom's right back where he started. He was doing good for a little while, but then he went back to his old prison cell."

Upon hearing this, Dave hurried to the middle of town to visit his old friend at the prison. When Dave entered, he had to hold his nose. Was this the same place? Was it possible that he'd lived *here*? Had it really been this bad? Dave was in disbelief.

"Tom?" Dave asked. "What are you doing here? Don't you remember that we were set free from this place?"

"But, man, you don't understand … When I left here, you wouldn't believe who I saw. Damian! Man, I know he was already a big guy, but somehow he grew. He's like ten feet tall now. He came up to me while I was walking down Straight Street and grabbed me by the throat! He threatened my life and threw me back in this place! No matter what, I'll never be free from him. I've tried, but he just keeps finding me. Every time that he throws me back in here, he grows taller and taller." Shaking his head, Tom put his hands over his face and cried.

Dave remembered the day he saw old Damian. "Come to think of it, I've seen him too."

"You did? So you know what I'm talkin' 'bout. I wonder how he got so much bigger," Tom replied.

Dave was a little puzzled. "What do you mean bigger? The first time I saw him after leaving here, he might have grown a little. I don't remember. I didn't pay too much attention to him. I kept reminding Damian of all of the things that were told to me by the visitor who set us free. Soon Damian began to get smaller and less intimidating. In fact, I saw him the other day, and I laughed at him! I couldn't believe that I had allowed him to trick me all those years. All that time spent sitting in this stinky, dark cell, and in reality, my bail had already been paid! Thomas, man, you've gotta get outta here!"

Tom became defensive. He accused Dave of being self-righteous and forgetting where he had come from. "How dare you lecture me? You don't understand! It was harder for me than it was for you. How dare you sit there and judge me?"

After going back and forth, Dave realized that his friend had already made up his mind. Dave bid his old friend farewell, and with a puzzled look, he shook his head in sorrow.

He left Tom sitting in the stinky, unlocked prison cell, still wearing the heavy, broken chains.

In the story of the two prisoners, Dave had a successful ending. Tom, however, wasn't so fortunate. Both prisoners were bound in chains, set free, and delivered. Both were forgiven for their past crimes and washed. Dave remained free, but Tom went back to a life of bondage. Both of these men were given freedom, but each handled his gift differently. To Dave, Damian appeared less intimidating.

Before these men were set free, something happened. They were offered salvation. It would be foolish of me to assume that just because you are reading this book, you have already been saved. What does it mean to be saved? Well, the definition is to be redeemed from sin and to be rescued from danger. It even means to be preserved or guarded from destruction or loss, or to be put aside as stored or reserved.

God sent His son, Jesus, to pay the price required for our sins. He paid the ultimate bond with His blood. It's like receiving a speeding ticket but learning that someone had paid the penalty before we even broke the law. It is left up to us to decide whether we will accept the pardon. God is able to pardon our offenses, no matter how bad, because the penalty was fulfilled through Jesus. If we would only believe that we have a savior, then we would be saved. This belief not only pardons us from all our crimes but also protects our goods from being confiscated and rescues us from capital punishment. If all that is not enough, belief in Him also promises a place of peaceful rest in His presence after we die.

When we make the decision to be saved, we become a part of God's family. The Bible tells us that He adopted us as His children. It is not a long, drawn-out process with paperwork and court dates.

> If you declare with your mouth, "Jesus is Lord," and believe in your heart that God raised Him from the dead, you will be saved. For it is with your heart that you believe and are justified, as it is with your mouth that you profess your faith and are saved. (Romans 10:9–10 NIV)

After confessing your faith in Jesus, it is important to find a church home that teaches the Word of God. Just as babies need to be nurtured after they are born, a new believer, being born again, needs to be led well. Baptism, which is important, follows salvation. You can read more about all these things in the Bible, which is the Word of God. It is very important to have a church home in which you can grow and develop, because we have an enemy that despises children of God. In a good church, you have the help of other family members and leaders to assist in guarding against the enemy. Just as in a natural family, some people complain about church families, but don't let that be your excuse for being a runaway. Get under a covering so that you have protection. The Lord wants you to be a part of His family, and if you've made the confession of faith in Jesus, the Bible tells us that all of heaven is rejoicing because of your decision.

> I tell you that in the same way there will be more rejoicing in heaven over one sinner who repents than over ninety-nine righteous persons who do not need to repent. (Luke 15:7 NIV)

For a new believer, this is the first day of your life! No longer a prisoner of sin, no longer sentenced to death—the crimes you were guilty of, whatever they are, have been paid for through the death and resurrection of our Savior, Jesus Christ. You have been set free!

In Matthew 13:3–8, Jesus tells the parable of the sower. When the sower went out to sow, some of his seed fell on different types of soil. In the story above, the Visitor spoke to Tom, just like the seed that fell along the road, but the accuser immediately came and took away the words of freedom. Dave was confronted by the accuser as well, but Dave, being good soil, remembered the Visitor and quoted His words to the accuser. Oftentimes, after leaving an unhealthy situation, we are immediately tempted to go right back to it. Whether the temptation comes by wooing and charming, or by outright intimidation and overpowering, it surely will come. We all must go through a time of testing. The important thing when going through these times is to remind the accuser of God's Word. The Word of God is the only weapon we have against Satan, and that is why it is called the Sword of the Spirit. We use that sword by opening our mouths and telling Satan what God's Word says.

You have value. God's desire is that no one would perish. But because He is love, He gives us the ability to choose either Him, the Good Shepherd, or your enemy, Satan. Many people put off the decision for salvation. But the truth is, making no decision *is* in fact a decision. Not choosing salvation through Christ Jesus our Lord is choosing to reject His gift of salvation and opting instead for death through Satan our enemy. On behalf of our

Father, my hope is that you've made the decision to believe in your heart and confess with your mouth Christ as Lord today.

But what about sin, habits, and addictions? If you are saved, aren't you also set free from the grip of Satan? Most Christians, if asked, would agree that they are indeed free. This issue of freedom doesn't quite make sense, though, because freedom and salvation go hand in hand. How can we be saved from sin and death yet be bound by it? How is it possible for a set-free child of God to be bound by Satan?

Great question! Let's explore this together. First let's take a look at the word *freedom*. What is freedom?

> Freedom is "the state of being free or at liberty rather than in confinement or under physical restraint: *He won his freedom after a retrial.*"
>
> Freedom is "exemption from external control, interference, regulation, etc."
>
> Freedom is "personal liberty, as opposed to bondage or slavery: a slave who bought his freedom."[1]

---

[1] Dictionary.com, s.v. "freedom," accessed September 1, 2022, https://www.dictionary.com/browse/freedom.

It is great to confess to be free from the bondage of sin, but how many truly are? It is likely that you or someone you know who is saved has an "issue" that they are dealing with. By "issue," I mean things like drugs, alcohol, smoking, pornography, gossiping or gambling. Physical handicaps are issues that may not always fall into this category in terms of how they are handled, for reasons that we will discuss later. These other "issues" that deal with sin, however, can hold us captive and prevent us from walking in the freedom that we have already been given. Different forms of bondage can require different approaches to walking in freedom. This is easy to understand if we consider the person bound by cigarettes in contrast to the one born deaf. Both individuals are bound by something debilitating, yet one issue was self-inflicted, while the other is the hand that was dealt, so to speak. In this study, we will be exploring solutions to gaining freedom from various forms of self-inflicted bondage, as well as avoiding the traps of becoming bound in the first place.

2

WHY THEN ARE PEOPLE BOUND?

Through Adam's sin, man has fallen. We, the seed of Adam, are sinful by nature because through the first man's sin we are under a curse.

This is easier to understand if we consider fruit. Within the fruit lies its seed, which holds the same genetic material as itself. We can understand that the seed inside the particular fruit will one day bear that same fruit. It would be foolish for us to expect different types of fruit to come from an apple seed. Just as a tree can produce only the fruit it came from, we human beings can produce only human beings. This is why the belief in evolution is utterly ridiculous. Man is sinful because we are from the seed of Adam.

Adam was made in the image of God, yet he chose to sin. When Adam sinned, he corrupted the seed of mankind. Being born from the family tree of Adam, we too are sinners by birth. Then comes the big "however":

> Therefore the Lord Himself will give you a sign: Behold, the virgin shall conceive and bear a Son, and shall call His name Immanuel. (Isaiah 7:14 NKJV)

It was important that Christ be born of a virgin, just as the prophecy said, because He must not come from the seed or body of man. He was born from a human, thus making him human, yet not from the seed of human beings, which would make Him cursed. Jesus did not know sin. Why? Because He was from the seed of God. Yet like us, He indeed was human. Born very lowly and yet as King, Jesus humbled Himself by leaving His heavenly throne and clothing Himself in mortal flesh. He was born to be a sacrifice for our sins.

Originally, the Israelites had to offer a lamb that was without defect or blemish to make atonement for their sin. This is why Jesus is called the Lamb of God (John 1:36 NKJV). He came to be the sacrifice to atone for our sin. In other words, He took our sins upon Himself and died in our place. Jesus only had to die once for our sin. He was raised from the dead and now lives forever. If we understand that He already died so that we can be free, it still leaves us with the question of why, then, believers are still living in bondage. The Word of God tells us that "if the Son sets you free, you will be indeed" (John 8:36 NIV). Jesus has stated that we are no longer bound because He, with His blood, has already paid the price for our freedom. If we have been set free, so that we are no longer bound, why then are so many still in bondage?

I've wrestled with this problem for many years and have noticed that there are differing reasons people remain in bondage. Let's explore these reasons one at a time. As you read, I invite you to examine your own life. If you are bound by something, whether by bad habits, an illness, or anything that holds you captive and causes you to feel like a prisoner, my prayer is that through this study you will take hold of your freedom, which was already paid in full with the blood of our Lord Jesus Christ. Amen.

SIN

Let's just put it right out there. There's no need for beating around the bush or sugarcoating the situation. One of the main reasons many people are in bondage is sin. Sin is the reason Adam's freedom was lost. Sin was the cause of Israel's captivity. Sin is the result of the godless state of our world. And sin is also the source of the bondage for many of the readers holding this book.

The Lord tells us throughout His Word to obey Him and keep His commands. As long as Israel was obedient, they were blessed. In the Complete Jewish Bible, Deuteronomy

28:1–14 warns Israel to fully obey the Lord's commands. If they remained obedient, they were promised blessings.

> "If you listen closely to what *Adonai* your God says, observing and obeying all his *mitzvot* [commandments] which I am giving you today, *Adonai* your God will raise you high above all the nations on earth; and all the following **blessings** [emphasis added here and following] will be yours in abundance—if you will do what *Adonai* your God says:
>
> "A **blessing** on you in the city, and a **blessing** on you in the countryside.
>
> "A **blessing** on the fruit of your body, the fruit of your land and the fruit of your livestock—the young of your cattle and flocks.
>
> "A **blessing** on your grain-basket and kneading-bowl.
>
> "A **blessing** on you when you go out, and a **blessing** on you when you come in.

"*Adonai* will cause your enemies attacking you to be defeated before you; they will advance on you one way and flee before you seven ways. *Adonai* will order a **blessing** to be with you in your barns and in everything you undertake; he will **bless** you in the land *Adonai* your God is giving you. *Adonai* will establish you as a people separated out for himself, as he has sworn to you—if you will observe the *mitzvot* of *Adonai* your God and follow his ways. Then all the peoples on earth will see that *Adonai*'s name, his presence, is with you; so that they will be afraid of you. *Adonai* will give you a great abundance of **good things**—of the fruit of your body, the fruit of your livestock and the fruit of your land in the land *Adonai* swore to your ancestors to give you. *Adonai* will open for you his **good treasure**, the sky, to give your land its rain at the right seasons and to bless everything you undertake. You will lend to many nations and not borrow; *Adonai* will make you the head and not the tail; and you will be only above, never below—if you

> will listen to, observe and obey the *mitzvot* of Adonai your God and not turn away from any of the words I am ordering you today, neither to the right nor to the left, to follow after other gods and serve them."

Notice how often the word "blessing" appears in this passage, along with "good things" and "good treasure." Blessings were promised to be everywhere they went and in all that they did.

This sounds a lot like parenting, or at least that's the way it is with my husband and me. If our children are careful to obey not some but *all* of our rules, they will be blessed. There would be no reason to keep any good thing from them. Obedient children are refreshing and a joy to give good things to. In fact, when they are doing well with their chores and schoolwork, I look for ways to bless them. However, if my children are misbehaving and slacking in things they are responsible for, it is not our favor they win but our wrath. A stubborn, hardheaded child is not at all delightful; they are not rewarded but punished.

Many of us want all the blessings promised in the above passage from Deuteronomy but have not kept God's commandments. God is a good Father; therefore, He does not reward evil with good. The rest of Deuteronomy 28 tells us what would happen if the Israelites were disobedient. In every place that the word *blessing* appears, it is replaced with the word *cursed*. In fact, the rest of the long chapter is filled with curses that will come upon those who are disobedient. The curses include skin disorders, diseases, insanity, blindness, slavery, even cannibalism—God warned the people that they would devour their own children in secret. Today in America, we are devouring our children by the millions. We have become so corrupt as a nation that this sin is no longer done in secret but is publicly announced over the airways! Abortion, once an unthinkable evil, has become embraced even by believers. Slavery in this country was the same way. In fact, the same argument was used as to why it was OK: the black man, just like the infant in the womb, was not thought of as being human and therefore as not deserving of rights. It took some time, but slavery was finally abolished in America. This gives us some hope for infants growing in the protective womb of their mothers.

Sin has a nasty way of corrupting a society. It tells us, the children of the Most High, that we should be free to do whatever we want. This is a trap, though, because sin enslaves its victims. Just as Adam corrupted his seed, we corrupt our seed even further by practicing sin. And in the case of abortion, we have eaten up our seed while it is in the process of growing and developing. We have announced to God that He has no say in our choices because whatever we feel is right *is* right! We sound like spoiled, ungrateful, rebellious teenagers. Sin clouds our thinking, corrupts our judgment, and focuses all of our attention on ourselves. Sin refuses to consider God and His Word. Sin is opposed to God and is therefore rooted in lies. Sin tells our Father, "I will do what I want to do! I know what's good for me! This makes me feel good, so I'll do it anyway!"

> Furthermore, just as they did not think it worthwhile to retain the knowledge of God, so God gave them over to a depraved mind, so that they do what ought not to be done. They have become filled with every kind of wickedness, evil, greed and depravity. They are full of envy, murder, strife, deceit and malice. They are gossips, slanderers, God-haters, insolent, arrogant and boastful; they invent ways of doing evil; they disobey their

> parents; they have no understanding, no fidelity, no love, no mercy. Although they know God's righteous decree that those who do such things deserve death, they not only continue to do these very things but also approve of those who practice them. (Romans 1:28–32 NIV)

When we give in to our own passions despite God's Word, we willingly hand over our mind to depravity. Just as a snowball grows when rolled in the snow, sin enlarges itself in our lives if we refuse to deal with it. Throughout scripture, we are warned that sin is a welcome mat for curses. Jeremiah warned Judah to repent for twenty-three years before Babylon took them captive. Yet they ignored God's call to repentance and continued in their evil ways (Jeremiah 25 NIV).

Have you ever dismissed someone's advice for you to straighten up and live right? Most of us have. We advise them to mind their own business, or we simply point out flaws we see in *their* lives. And if you've never done these things, well … most of us have. But it's not them being in our business that we're really worried about. It has more to do with our desire to keep doing the things that we are doing.

However, it is important for us to remember history. After being warned again and again, Judah, just like Israel, went into captivity. The children of Israel are God's chosen people. They have been set apart from all of the people on the earth as His own. Speaking as a Gentile believer, I know that I have been adopted into the Family through Christ. He loves us as His own children; however, we have been reminded and warned not to be boastful for we have been grafted into the Family. If God punishes His natural children and was willing to give them over to slavery, why should He not do the same to those who have been adopted? Whether the captivity is natural or spiritual, the punishment still applies. But just because the Lord's children, whether Jew or Gentile, fall into sin, which leads to bondage, it doesn't mean we have to remain that way.

> If my people, who are called by my name, will humble themselves and pray and seek my face and turn from their wicked ways, then I will hear from heaven, and I will forgive their sin and will heal their land. (2 Chronicles 7:14 NIV)

By the grace of God, America no longer practices slavery. We now see slavery as sin, and we are ashamed to have tolerated such a dishonor of human life. This same dishonor, however, has shown itself in other ways. Yet we must remain hopeful—hopeful that we as a nation will turn back to God and once again follow after His ways.

FOR THE LORD'S GLORY

There are, however, times that people are in bondage due to no fault of their own. Sometimes people are bound so God can receive glory. Bondage takes on many forms, one of which is blindness. In John 9, Jesus's disciples asked about the man who was born blind. They wondered whose fault it was that he was born blind, his or his parents'. Their question made sense, considering that sin brings bondage. However, Jesus answered them that "His blindness is due neither to his sin nor to that of his parents; it happened so that God's power might be seen at work in him" (John 9:3 CJB). This man had been blind his whole life, so God would be glorified from him being healed. Therefore, we must not assume that we or others are carrying a burden that was brought on by sin. As it was with this man, sin is not always the reason.

Job was robbed of his wealth, children, health, and even status in a single day. But unlike most, Job was blameless and upright. No one could claim that Job was being punished because of his sins or for some fault on his behalf. His friends did assume that it was Job's fault, but they were very wrong. Satan was the one bringing all the disaster on Job. He was allowed to do so with God's permission only. The Lord not only allowed but invited Satan to attack Job, knowing that Job was up for the challenge.

When I first read the story of Job, I didn't understand why God would put Job out there like that. Satan didn't even mention Job—God did. When I read this, I initially saw it as God putting Job in harm's way by giving everything that Job owned into the hands of Satan. At that time in my life, I would have felt betrayed if I were Job. But Job, when the messengers came and told him of all that he had lost, even his children, fell down and worshipped God!

Imagine, if you will, a boxing coach who is also the proud father of a great young boxer. He not only welcomes but invites opponents to fight his son. The father, who has been a coach to many talented boxers for years, has been watching his son train and had never seen anyone quite like him. Watching his son train with such excellence and diligence produces a firm confidence in this young man that the coach hadn't had in other fighters. Surely, this boy has a devotion unlike any other. *I know that he can face anyone!* The father then proves his confidence in his son by setting up a fight with the most vicious opponent he can find, all the while sure of the victory that will be won by the prized son. The father's confidence in the victory to be won by his son is not reckless but honorable.

I believe that there are still upright and blameless people, and yes, even perfect people. Jesus even tells us in Matthew 5:48 (NIV) to be perfect just as our Father in heaven is perfect. He says this after giving us some pretty firm commands. The cliché goes "Well, nobody's perfect." But the Word of God says, "Be thou perfect." As children of God, it is vital that we remember to speak the things that the Lord tells us, not what the world says. It may not be popular, but it is honorable to speak and believe God's Word above all else.

Job's friends thought what most of us would have thought. "No one is punished for no reason. God punishes the wicked, not the righteous. Who can be righteous but God?" All of this sounds right, but it had nothing to do with what God was doing or allowing to be done to Job. God was not punishing

Job as it seemed. He was allowing Satan to afflict him for a time. And yes, our righteousness is as filthy rags, and none is righteous—no, not one. How then was Job righteous? And if it is unattainable, why does Jesus tell us to be perfect just as our Father is perfect? Well, it's simply this: in myself—that is, in my flesh—nothing good dwells. But there is something greater at work within me. We have a oneness with our Father through Christ by His Holy Spirit that lives in us. We have been made righteous because our Father is righteous. The more we follow after and become one with the Lord, the more we begin to look and act like Him. Therefore, Jesus can tell us to be perfect just as our heavenly Father is perfect.

There were people in history who didn't live in sin. Yes, they were born in sin, but they refused to allow it to keep them in bondage to sin. They did not allow their circumstances to dictate the type of person they would become. Job said that he had made a covenant with his eyes not to look at a young woman. He even said that if he was guilty of such a thing, then may his wife sleep with another man. Job was not prideful; he just knew that he was not a sinful man, and therefore he did not allow his friends to accuse him.

In the book of Job, the Lord allows Job to lose all that he had and then restores all that was lost with an increase.

If Job had lost nothing, there would be no story. Job would have been OK with what he had, which was good. But God brought Job, perfect Job, blameless and upright Job, even higher. Job went through more in one day than many of us will ever experience in a lifetime. Yet Job came out of the fire as pure gold. There may be times in our lives when we don't understand why we have to go through certain things. But we must keep our eyes on the Lord, trusting and believing that He is working all things together for our good.

Joseph also faced some hardship. His brothers hated him and wanted to kill him. But they decided it would be more profitable to make some money by selling him as a slave to some distant family members instead. Those family members did a "flip" and made a profit by reselling him to slave owners in another country.

After being purchased by an Egyptian, he was put in charge of everything the Egyptian owned. Things seemed to be getting better, until the wife of his master had other plans for the young man. She saw how handsome Joseph was and tried to seduce him. But because Joseph was an excellent young man, he honored his master by not giving in to her desire. Joseph was not rewarded for this; instead he was accused of attempted rape and thrown in prison.

Joseph, an honorable young man, was bound by slavery inflicted first by his own brothers. Still bound, he was sold again by distant relatives to the Egyptian. Then after being falsely accused, he was thrown into prison. Joseph was repeatedly bound. He was not guilty of sin in any of these cases, yet he was bound. But even in all the turmoil Joseph went through, God had a plan. Joseph had to be in Egypt at the correct time. Slavery and prison were just paths to get him there. Because Joseph was in prison, he met Pharaoh's baker and cupbearer. This meeting led to his freedom and promotion by Pharaoh. Joseph, like Christ, became a savior. Joseph saved both Egypt and his own family, the very same family who had sold him into slavery.

Had he stayed in the comfort of his father's house, he and all his family would have died out from the famine that came upon the land. No one knew any of these details, but God foreknew the time and details of everything that would take place. Therefore, God allowed Joseph to be bound for a time, just as Christ would be at a later date. After the time of doom was over, both Joseph's and Jesus's restoration and promotion brought about salvation for many.

Many years later, Israel became enslaved in Egypt for no fault of their own. The new pharaoh didn't know Joseph and was intimidated by Israel's greatness. (He sounds a lot like Joseph's brothers.) He therefore enslaved the people of Israel and even murdered their little boys (Exodus 1:6–22). But this too was allowed to bring glory to God. Moses was raised up to bring judgment on Egypt and to set the Lord's people free. (Exodus 3:10). People from all around feared God and His people after seeing the fate of Egypt for afflicting the Lord's people (Exodus 15:14–16).

Only God can see all of the details that we cannot. Therefore, although it may be tempting to be angry with our Lord, it is important that we trust in Him, knowing that no matter how bad things appear to be, God sees all and is always in control. There are certain things that we must go through, certain places we must endure, and certain people that we must encounter in order to bring about God's will on earth. Job had to endure it, as did Joseph, but their latter days were greater than the early ones. Unfortunately, Israel complained about their hardships throughout their desert experience and kept looking back on their time as slaves in Egypt. They complained against Moses and God and repeatedly sinned. For these reasons, they did not enter into the fullness of God's promises. That generation died in the wilderness, and their children went instead into the promised land.

Even if our bondage is no fault of our own, we must still guard ourselves against complaining. We must not fall into "woe is me" as most people do when faced with uncomfortable challenges in life. It is up to us to respond well. Our goal should be to respond with humility and reverence, knowing that our Father is in control of everything. Any other response is prideful, arrogant, and disrespectful. Being angry and complaining about necessary prison cells only proves to be foolish, immature, and spoiled rotten.

Paul, when in prison, sang praises to God, not praises to his problem (Acts 16:25 NIV). He could have sung the old "Why me?" hymn that most of us sing when things look bad, but he praised the Lord instead. We are told to rejoice if we are counted worthy to suffer for the sake of Christ, for we will be blessed (1 Peter 4:12–15 NIV). What hold does the enemy have when he can't shake our faith? None!

Not only was he in prison, but Paul also had what he referred to as a thorn in his side. It is unclear what this thorn was, specifically, but it is clear that it was not at all comfortable. If it weren't troublesome, he would not have begged the Lord three times to remove it. But God's response was not what we might expect. His response to Paul was simply, "My grace is enough for you, for My power is brought to perfection in weakness" (2 Corinthians 12:9 CJB). Many believers are unfortunately not OK with this type of response. But in reality we, like Paul, ought to count it all as joy if this is what we are told, knowing and trusting that God is sovereign. We are invited to rest in His assurance that no matter the outcome of our affliction, we can trust in His omnipotent and perfect will. After the Lord's response, Paul says that for Christ's sake, he delights in weaknesses, insults, hardships, persecutions, and difficulties, for it is when he is weak that he is strong (2 Corinthians 2:10 NIV). If you're bound by something, ask the Lord to set you free from it! If the bondage is the result of sin, repent and be set free by the saving grace of God.

However, if the bondage you are dealing with is from no fault of your own, then learn from the examples that scripture gives. The Lord gave us Paul, Job, and many others as examples to model after. The ultimate example is Christ. He always spoke what God spoke and did what God did. He mirrored the Father in all things. When it was time for His body to be given over to death, for a time Jesus asked the Father if there could be another way. Then in the same prayer, he cried, "Not My will, but Your will be done" (Luke 22:42 NIV).

There are differences between burdens from Satan and

burdens from the Lord. The Lord has already assured us that His burden is light. But know this for sure: to whom much is given, much is required. Paul had the weight of being in the very presence of Greatness. He'd visited the third heaven where God dwells. When attempting to write about this experience, he not only referred to himself in the third person for the sake of remaining humble but also lacked the words to describe the Awesomeness of that which he beheld. Human language lacks the capacity even to begin to express the things he saw in the vision. Let's just say that Paul, in his humble state, needed to be given something to be kept low. Paul understood this, and after begging for "freedom" from this "thorn," he accepted God's answer and remained humble (2 Corinthians 12:2–10 NIV).

Job's burdens were also from Satan, and in the end he was not only restored but received a double portion from the Lord (Job 42:10 NIV). So understand that if you are afflicted due to no fault of your own, patience is key. Know and trust that there is a great purpose for your temporary state of affliction. Some people will be set free in this lifetime. Others, like Paul, may be refused healing by God. They may spend the rest of their physical lives afflicted. Their deliverance will come after being raised to eternal life with Christ.

ADDICTION

> **addiction** *noun*
>
> the state of being enslaved to a habit or practice or to something that is psychologically or physically habit-forming, as narcotics, to such an extent that its cessation causes severe trauma.[2]

In the story I shared about the two prisoners, we see that Dave and Tom struggled with addiction. This fictional story may seem a bit unlikely, but it is the serious and sad reality for many. In life, there are some Daves, people who have been set free from a life of bondage and are made new. Unfortunately, though, there are also Toms, who believe that they will never truly be free. Addiction has many faces: alcohol, lust, poverty, drugs, gambling, homosexuality, gossip, fornication, tobacco, gluttony, even exercise. Whatever the addiction, the important thing is to be free from any and all of them.

As previously stated, addiction is the state of being enslaved by something or some habit. If you are suffering from

---

[2] Dictionary.com, s.v. "addiction," accessed September 2, 2022, https://www.dictionary.com/browse/addiction.

a compulsive disorder, you are enslaved to the compulsions of the disorder. The very word "disorder" tells us that something is not in order in a person's life. In most if not all of these cases, the addict is entertaining a demon or is being held captive by demonic oppression. I've heard people say that the best lie Satan tells is that he doesn't exist. If we believe that he doesn't exist or is not at work in our lives, he can more freely reign over us.

Both Tom and Dave were held captive and being oppressed by Damian. Both men were also set free when the Visitor came into their cell and broke their chains. Likewise, we were set free from whatever demon that has held us captive. We were set free by the blood of Jesus, who already paid our bond by dying on the cross for our sins. He set us free, and like Dave, we are free indeed! It is very important that we not allow Satan and his demons to seduce us back into bondage, making a mockery of Christ's sacrifice. It may be a struggle to resist the enemy, but each of us has the ability to do so. James 4:7 (NKJV) tells us, "Therefore submit to God. Resist the devil and he will flee from you." Damian choked Tom and threw him back in the prison. Yet when he approached Dave, he left him alone until another time. And each time after that, he had to flee because Dave's response to Damian was different from Tom's. Both men were bound, both were set free, and both were tempted. It was their response to their enemy that determined their outcome.

> How blessed is the man who perseveres through temptation! For after he has passed the test, he will receive as his crown the Life which God has promised to those who love him. No one being tempted should say, "I am being tempted by God." For God cannot be tempted by evil, and God himself tempts no one. Rather, each person is being tempted whenever he is being dragged off and enticed by the bait of his own desire. Then, having conceived, the desire gives birth to sin; and when sin is fully grown, it gives birth to death. (James 1:12–15 CJB)

Temptation has authority over us only if we secretly want it to. We see this in the example of Christ when tempted by Satan. Satan tried to tempt Jesus with food to feed and please his weary flesh after fasting for forty days and being hungry. He also tried to offer Jesus power and authority in exchange for worshiping him. Satan then tried to convince Jesus to test God by putting Himself in jeopardy. Each time Satan tried to tempt Jesus, he slickly and cunningly quoted scripture. However, Jesus, the very Word of God, responded with the same Words in the correct context (Luke 4:1–13 NIV). Satan is a snake, and if we are not careful to study the Word of God, we can easily be tempted and led astray. It is important for us to understand that the Holy Spirit will remind us of the scripture that is needed at the appointed time (John 14:26 NIV). This example that Jesus provides us with reinforces the truth that temptation has no authority over us if we don't desire it. We are also promised that whenever we are tempted, the Lord always provides a way out (1 Corinthians 10:13 NIV). And God is not a man that He should lie! Like our parents, the Lord gets rid of all of our excuses.

I hear too often of people hiding behind the excuse of having an addiction. Yes, I said it! When it comes to addiction, it's as if there's some weird rule that we are not allowed to declare to those that are held captive, "Be free!" Somehow, the addict is given a pass to continue in sin and bondage. Yet I boldly declare to you that even addiction has no power over the blood that Christ has already shed! Amen.

Satan's lies that he tells an addict about themselves are

things like "I just can't stop" or "I have no power over it." Yet the man or woman with the pornography addiction has the ability to stop while in the presence of others. Likewise, I've known many drug addicts yet have never witnessed the "ceremony" of worship to the destruction of their own bodies. Even smokers are forced to restrain from doing so inside public buildings. It seems obvious that if an addict can refrain from performing self-destructive rituals until they are able to indulge, they have much more self-control than they may be willing to admit.

I've referred to these indulgences as a ceremony of worship, because that's exactly what it is. Consider the purpose behind the high that is attained or sought after when a child of God pollutes themselves. The captive's primary concern is to bring the mind and body to a place beyond reality. Have you ever been in a worship service and raised your hands in adoration and praise to God? When we worship, nothing or no one else matters. It's all about giving honor to the Lord. Likewise, addiction takes its victim beyond the everyday. Instead of adoration and honor to God, the adoration goes to the abuser, and this does not lead to honor but to dishonor. The addict does not take anyone or anything else into consideration. They don't care whom they hurt, as long as they are able to have their own flesh satisfied and indulged. This is the opposite of love, because love doesn't seek its own. When we worship God, it causes us to love others and even esteem them above ourselves. Self-worship desires only self-esteem and gives no thought or concern to others. It devalues our Lord and His other children who were made in His image. Like the pride of Lucifer, it declares, "I am to be exalted! I will lift myself up on high!"

There is unfortunately a false hope that exists in the body of believers. Many addicts are waiting on God to show up, touch them in a miraculous way, and BOOM!—they are free from bondage! Well, here's the truth: not only is that false hope, but it makes Christ's sacrifice null and void. This expectation mocks the cross because by His blood we have already been set free. Jesus, by His sacrificial death and resurrection, has already paid the price for our freedom. He also took the keys of death, destruction, and bondage from our enemy! Since Satan no longer holds the keys to the chains that he lays on God's children, we don't have to keep them on!

Addiction is a sickness that is passed down from generation to generation. It takes on many forms. For some people, it may be drugs; for others, overconsumption of alcohol, or maybe gambling. I've heard people constantly brag about the fact that they don't drink or smoke when the topic of family curses involving addiction is discussed. However, as stated previously, addiction is the state of being *enslaved to a habit or practice* or to something that is psychologically or physically habit-forming, such as narcotics, to such an extent that its cessation causes severe trauma.

I've noticed a trend in our society in which very many people are addicted to improper relationships. I know of very few people who are not in a relationship that involves a "significant other." These others are usually referred to as "friends." Even new divorcees go from the courtroom straight into courting again in no time at all. We human beings change "friends" like we change clothes. Some insist that this time it's different: "This is the one!" Others simply shrug it off casually as just having a little fun. As a result, children are the fruit of sleeping around with multiple lovers, and half brothers and half sisters have multiple mothers and fathers. These children grow up thinking that this is what a normal family looks like, thus producing more and more abnormal and sinful institutions that are now accepted as a "family." A family consists of one man, one woman, and if the Lord is willing, children. In America, this picture is becoming more and more distorted—even to the extent of "family" consisting of two women or even multiple men. When we begin to redefine what God has instituted as a family, the true family disappears, and false ones emerge.

Growing up, I noticed things about the world around me that I didn't like. I noticed the problem of addiction running wild. Addictions ranged from drugs and alcohol to lust and godlessness. I wondered if I even had a chance! I remember always wanting children, lots of them. But I was uninterested in marriage because I rarely saw examples of good ones. My first year of marriage was rough—actually, the first few years. I always planned and expected Donald to leave. He knew this and reassured me constantly that I was stuck with him because he wasn't going anywhere. Had Donald thought the same as I had, our marriage wouldn't have lasted through the first year. My heart breaks for married couples going through divorce, because I understand the struggles to hold on and keep working at it. Malachi 2:16 (NIV) says that "the man who hates and divorces his wife does violence to the one he should protect." In certain areas of our marriage, I am the strong one, while in other areas Donald is. When the Lord unites two people, it is the duty of each person to strengthen the other. Just as iron sharpens iron, we must assist and build each other up, helping the other where there is a weakness.

Addiction is a trap, and it makes us careful to protect each other as well as our children from the temptations and traps from the enemy.

If Satan has a stronghold of addiction on you or your family, it's time for him to let you go! We have a Savior who has already paid the price for our freedom! Temptation will come; everyone experiences it. But as we continue to stand upon the Word of God, keeping and remembering His promises to us, we begin to realize that we are already victorious. Remember that our enemy walks around like a roaring lion looking for lives that he can eat up. He has eaten away at so many through lies. Addiction can cause people to believe that they will never be anything more than what they appear to be today. "You've tried quitting before! Don't you remember? Just face it—you'll always be an alcoholic!" Or you may have heard "You'll never amount to anything! Stop trying, you're wasting time!" Or maybe this one: "You were born a homosexual. That is who you are and who you always will be. Don't try to change—you're fine just the way you are!" Knowing that there is a lion roaming about, we need always to be on guard and armed with our Sword, which is the Word of God!

There are things that we don't consider about addictions.

They don't just start by themselves—they have to be developed. We have to start doing something repetitively until it catches on, like a habit. Some habits get rolling pretty quickly, while others have to be repeated over and over before they catch on. Whatever is practiced frequently will pick up momentum and eventually gain strength. When addiction has a grip over a life, it is because the activity has been exercised, fed, and nurtured. I think that it's amazing we have the ability to choose what becomes strong and dominate! Whatever thing or things we spend time practicing or studying will gain the most influence in our lives. We have the power and ability to choose what we feed ourselves. Feeding on things that our flesh craves will help to strengthen worldly lusts and corrupt desires, while feeding on the Word of God strengthens our inner man, the one who lives eternally!

Before my husband and I were married, we began to engage in premarital sex. As a Christian, I knew that this was wrong. But for some reason, I kept doing it. It was as if a battle was going on between my spirit, which wanted to please my Father, and my flesh, which wanted to please me. Unfortunately, my flesh seemed to win the war each time, leaving me feeling as if I had betrayed my King yet again. There is a deep feeling of filthiness and shame that overshadows a child of God after committing acts that are disgraceful. It is lonely, scary, and leaves the victim feeling dirty. This feeling drew me away from the closeness I had once had with God. My relationship with God wasn't perfect before my sinful act, but it was much healthier than it had become. But now I had *willingly* sinned, and not only that, I had become a repeat offender! I claimed to love God, and yet here I was totally defying His instructions for me to flee from sin. Instead of fleeing, I had embraced it! My commitment was originally to Him only. I had now committed my body to sin. I felt like a hypocrite. As a result, I eventually stopped going to church and felt unworthy to witness to others.

But *why* did I continue to do this? It made no sense! If the Word is true that "He Who is in me is greater than he who is in the world," why then was I still stuck? I did not realize that I was the one determining the outcome of the battle I had been fighting. It was all about my diet—well, not naturally, but spiritually. Sure, I read my Bible, thus feeding my Spirit. But I didn't realize that I fed my flesh way more with secular music. In high school, I listened to lots of R & B, most of which talked about fornication. It played while I slept, it played in everyone's car I rode in, and even when the radio was not on, it played in my head. I had unwittingly practiced and mastered this way of thinking and living. My music choices were in direct opposition to the Word of God. Because I fed on both the secular world and the Word of God, my flesh was constantly at war with the Holy Spirit in me.

> Those who keep sowing in the field of their old nature, in order to meet its demands, will eventually reap ruin; but those who keep sowing in the field of the Spirit will reap from the Spirit everlasting life. (Galatians 6:8 CJB)

Despite the message everyone tried to comfort me with—that my sin was somehow OK with God—I knew better. The Holy Spirit within me convicted me of my continued sin and called me to live a life that was honorable. I knew that despite the messages of grace I had heard my whole life, it just didn't seem right to continue living a life of sin while claiming to be "free." Romans 6:1–2 (CJB) says,

> So then, are we to say, "Let's keep on sinning, so that there can be more grace"? Heaven forbid! How can we, who have died to sin, still live in it?"

The fear of the Lord caused me to flee from my sinful lifestyle. Donald and I married and were relieved to live a life that mirrored our faith. I always had a love for music, but when I began to realize the dark hold it held over my life, I knew that it had to go! Gradually things like my choices in movies and even books began to change. I began to notice that the more worldly weight I shed, the more spiritual muscle I would gain. The things that once tempted me were now disgusting to me. God gave me a fervor for things that are holy and pure, as He washed me clean from the things that were causing me so much grief.

It's strange now for me to think back on how much I had loved secular music. By the grace of God, I no longer love or desire any part of it. I can now see how Satan was so easily able to minister to me through my love of music. The words of the music that I'd listened to reminded me of how good it feels to be held, cherished, desired, wanted, and adored. I had traded my worship of God for self-worship. What I was practicing was purely demonic, and its influence over my life was dark and depressing, literally luring me out of the presence of the Lord.

If you struggle with lust of any kind, take time out to take an honest look at things in your life that are influencing you. What is it that takes your time? Take an honest survey of your influences, and search for anything that may be hindering your spiritual growth. For some, it might be movies, magazines, books, music, even friends. It is important to hold these influences up to the light of God's Word. If the lyrics, the message, the language, or even the heart of it doesn't line up with His Word, kick it out of your life! Fill up that empty space with His Word and with spiritual songs that give glory to the only One deserving of our worship.

> For the rest, brethren, whatever is true, whatever is worthy of reverence and is honorable and seemly, whatever is just, whatever is pure, whatever is lovely and lovable, whatever is kind and winsome and gracious, if there is any virtue and excellence, if there is anything worthy of praise, think on and weigh and take account of these things [fix your minds on them]. Practice what you have learned and received and heard and seen in me, and model your way of living on it, and the God of peace (of untroubled, undisturbed well-being) will be with you. (Philippians 4:8–9 AMPC)

This gives us the secret to God's peace. Fixing the mind on good things washes and sanctifies our way of thinking. Meditating, focusing, and fixing the mind or soul on that which is good and honorable not only feeds but nourishes the soul. When your soul is well nourished, it can and will flourish! In just the same way addictions begin, by practice good habits are formed and developed.

FOOLISHNESS

Information saves lives. The Word tells us that people are destroyed for lack of knowledge (Hosea 4:6 NKJV). There is a Bible in almost every home in America, yet it is rarely read. There are places where people are hungry for the Word of God, so hungry that they are willing to die for it. They understand that in it lies truth, freedom, secrets, and even the very heart of God. Yet here in America it goes unread, unstudied, and unopened.

The Word of God holds the solution to all things. With the wisdom that it teaches, life just begins to make sense. Studying God's Word will save your life! Many people are not aware that all they have to do is resist the devil. Many are so overwhelmed by the sight of the enemy that they fail to consider God's power over him. If the Lord's people only knew the power that we have over our enemy! Isaiah 14 speaks of the way in which we will look at the enemy.

> Those who see you will stare at you,
> reflecting on what has become of you:
> 'Is this the man who shook the earth,
> who made kingdoms tremble,
> who made the world a desert,
> who destroyed its cities,
> who would not set his prisoners free?'
> (Isaiah 14:16–17 CJB)

Sure, people are bound by physical things, but there are also things that can hold us captive in our mind. The way in which we think can and will affect our lives in every way. Our thinking is mostly the result of our environment. When we consider how we argue with one another, we can see that each person is absolutely, positively right! If only we could just get this other person to understand and see the truth. We all strongly believe that we are right. Fortunately, though, someone has to be wrong. Being wrong about something is not welcomed by most of us. We hold to certain beliefs and opinions as if we're holding on for dear life. Mostly it's because it's all we know as truth.

A presidential election was going on, and as a child, I foolishly commented on a candidate while a commercial was on. A lady I had a lot of respect for heard my comment and spoke one sentence to me that has stayed with me ever since and forever changed my way of thinking. She politely responded, "Crystal, you don't vote a certain way just because of the color of your skin." I was shocked and amazed. How embarrassing and humbling to realize that my mind had been programmed to think in a prejudiced and close-minded way. People around me spoke a certain way, and just because this was what I was used to, I accepted it as truth! When I grew up, both physically and spiritually, I began to see things more clearly. Praise God for a word spoken in love! Had I not gotten that word when I did, I'd be believing and even supporting things just because everyone around me did, and not because the Lord does.

When I got older, I began to research what we are really voting for when we choose a liberal or conservative candidate. The results left me shocked and amazed. There I sat in front of my computer with my heart broken. If I was not challenged to think differently as a child, I would've grown up with twisted reasoning. And now I think of all of the countless others who have not been told or still hold to the same prejudiced ways of thinking as the people in their circle. It is time for us as believers to wake up and remove the blinders from our eyes. It is as if Satan has been singing a lullaby to the Lord's people, and we've been closing our eyes to truth and accepting lies as an alternative.

> Woe to those who call evil good
> and good evil,
> who change darkness into light
> and light into darkness,
> who change bitter into sweet
> and sweet into bitter!
> Woe to those seeing themselves as wise,
> esteeming themselves as clever. (Isaiah 5:20 CJB)

It's amazing that Satan is able to get away with the things that he gets away with, without the Lord's children suspecting a thing. He has a way of hiding things in plain sight and is still able to fool so many. It is as if he does it to mock us for our lack of discernment and unwillingness to pay attention to detail. Scripture uses directional references to teach us about spiritual truths. We are told that the Son sits at the right hand of the Father. Likewise, when a father blessed his children, he would place his right hand on his son's head and pray a blessing upon him (Genesis 48:14 NKJV).

There is also a left and a right wing in our country. Socially, the left supports things like gay marriage and abortion, and the right does not. I think that it is interesting that the right supports future generations as well as the family structure, in just the same way as the blessing was passed down from the right hand of the father. In our English language, we even use the word "right" to teach and convey that which is correct and acceptable. If anyone dares to stand up and call the slaughtering of infants in the womb evil, they are themselves accused of being evil and denying freedom to the poor and afflicted mother who should have the right to murder her child if it pleases her or makes her life more comfortable. If one dares to speak the Word of God, declaring that homosexuality is indeed sin, they are bullied by America and its citizens for daring to bring God into our country! The left wants the name of God, along with anything with scripture on it, to be removed and simply erased from our buildings or anything that represents America. How could I have been zealous for standing on the wrong side of the line just because I was told that it was the good side? Scripture warns of a woe to those who call evil good and good evil.

My heart breaks for our land, for our sins are so many. We have been zealous for evil, and we even speak up in support of lawlessness. I've often wondered how much longer it will be before our Father has had enough of our cruelty. We have been foolishly allowing the lies of Satan to sway our very ways of thinking. We have held on to political and world views as if they were the very words of God. Foolishly, we have supported depravity, injustice, and lawlessness without taking the time to ask our Lord His view through His Word.

It seems unreal. The passion we Americans, even we Christians, have for supporting an agenda that outright attacks the family is just unbelievable! How can this be? How can so many of us be fooled into following after evil? The answer is found in the Word of God. "Foolishness," the Word tells us, "is bound up in the heart of a child; the rod of correction will drive it far from him" (Proverbs 22:15 NKJV). We all have times in our lives in which we must receive correction, but thank God for it.

> The rod and rebuke give wisdom, but a child left to himself brings shame on his mother. (Proverbs 29:15 CJB)

Most of us don't enjoy being corrected. It hurts our pride. But the reward of humbling ourselves and submitting to reproof is wise.

Our ignorance of God's Word causes us not only to be an easy target but also a victim of bondage from our enemy. It is not easy for Satan to trick us when we know and understand our Father. The way we get to know Him is by studying His Word. We can see this in our relationships.

My husband and I study each other very closely to have a better way of responding to each other. We observe facial cues, body language, volume, tone, and pitch. This watching and observing started before we were married and has not stopped. The closer we become, the more we want to know about each other. When we spend time with people we love, we begin to *know* them. Most women are enraged with their husbands because the husband's response in an argument is "I didn't know that would make you mad! I can't read your mind!" Unfortunately, neither of them has taken enough time to study the other. If they had, he'd at least be able to discern that his wife is in some type of distress, and over time he may be able to tell her what's bothering her before she even knows. If the wife had done her homework and studied her husband, she'd know that at certain parts of the day, his patience is shorter. This will help clue her in to when to be frank and when to be mysterious.

Most of us are just not willing to spend the time to study. But if you love someone, If you are truly passionate about them, you will study them. One Valentine's Day before my husband and I were married, I came home from school and found a huge red gift bag on my bed. Donald had stopped by and left it for my mother to put it there. Inside the bag was the attention he'd paid to me: a bunch of little everyday things that I used and liked, practical things like lotions and favorite things like chocolates. I was overwhelmed! I couldn't believe how much attention he'd paid to the little things about me. That day, I knew that he was the man I wanted to be my husband.

Likewise, we are married to God. As the bride of Christ, how much have you studied Him? In Jewish culture, there is a better understanding of studying a person. What we understand as a disciple is referred to as a *talmid* (disciple). Talmidim didn't just listen to their rabbi speak and memorize the lessons taught by them. A talmid was more of a son than a mere student. The relationship of rabbi and talmid has been described by a common saying: "just as one candle lights another only if it is brought close, so a Rabbi only teaches well when he is close to his Talmidim."[3] The authors go on to describe the relationship as being closer and more intimate than that of a father and son. The talmid copied everything the rabbi said and did, even down to his mannerisms and habits. Just as a child copies a parent, so also the talmid copy his rabbi. Therefore, our translation of these terms as "teacher" and "disciple" leaves us with little understanding. The talmid left behind everything and everyone to follow in the path of his rabbi. In a sense, I might say that he *became* his rabbi. They did everything together and shared a bond that was not easily broken. Jesus's talmidim had this type of relationship with Him. Wherever He slept, they slept; wherever He ate, they ate; and wherever He led, they followed.

When He was in the garden of Gethsemane before being taken to be beaten and crucified, Jesus, in agony to the point of death, asked His talmidim, "Couldn't you watch with Me for one hour?" He asked His talmidim, the ones He'd loved,

---

[3] Ann Spangler and Lois Tverberg, *Sitting at the Feet of Rabbi Jesus*, (Grand Rapids, Michigan: Zondervan, 2009), p. 59.

to watch and pray with Him. Instead they slept. Upon His return, He asked them to stay awake, keep watch, and pray for just one hour. Each time He returned, He found them sleeping. I cannot begin to imagine the agony of Christ. He was sorrowful to the point of death, and even after repeatedly asking his closest and dearest talmidim, the men with whom He had eaten, taught, and lived for His entire ministry, to watch and pray, He found them asleep (Matthew 26:36–43 NIV). These men, the Lord's beloved, had been overcome by fatigue. Instead of being there for their rabbi when He needed them most, they were asleep.

The last time He woke them up, they realized how important the need to be alert had been. Judas, one of the twelve, approached with a kiss of betrayal. Jesus was now in the hands of the enemy, betrayed by one of His own. Judas led the way to his rabbi in exchange for what he truly loved: money.

What is it you love? What are you passionate about? Is it something, or someone? Is it Christ? Most people will quickly respond, "Yes! I'm passionate about Jesus!" without even giving it much thought. Well, if you really want to be honest, just ask yourself what you are giving your time to study. What do you do for more than an hour every day? Is it TV, the internet, a relationship, talking on the phone, texting, browsing through videos, or studying the Word of God? "Where your treasure is, there your heart will be also" (Matthew 6:21 KNJV). Whatever we spend our time studying is the area in which we will grow and mature.

> When I was a child, I talked like a child, I thought like a child, I reasoned like a child. When I became a man, I put the ways of childhood behind me. (1 Corinthians 13:11 NIV)

Moving on to maturity enables us to fight the good fight. When Satan tempted Jesus in the wilderness, Jesus responded with the Word of God each and every time. Satan was unsuccessful in leading Christ astray simply because Jesus confessed and stood upon the Word of God!

Many people are losing their battle with the enemy simply because they are ignorant of God's Word. Not knowing that we are on the winning team causes people to tap out and give up right before the big KO! How differently would we live our lives if we knew and understood that we actually win? Whether you are an adult or a child spiritually, Satan still walks about like a roaring lion seeking whom he may devour. I commission you to grow up! Study the One that you say you love! Be a child no longer, and stand firm on the word of God!

The other day we were all sitting in the living room after church, and my children asked if they could have a doughnut. The doughnuts were sitting on the table in the back room. "Go ahead," I said, and off they raced. Not one of them hesitated! It would have been silly not to go and get it. Can you imagine them asking and then sitting there on the couch, waiting for me to say it again? Or worse, waiting for me to get a beautiful lace doily, place the doughnut directly in the center, and serve each of them with a tall glass of cold creamy milk? Of course not! Those kids got up and ran to get the prize! Are you hungry? And if so, just how hungry are you?

3

DO YOU WANT TO BE FREE? A-S-K!

There is a difference between what we say and what we do. Have you ever wanted all As in school but refused to study? Or what about a shiny new sports car? Well, where is all of the cash you've saved? What is the plan to actually get it? Anytime I've said that I want something, my husband begins planning ways for me to attain it, so I must be very careful. Donald gets out a pad of paper and a pen when the kids or I have a goal that we want to reach. He writes down the vision so that we are able to run with it. Just passively saying ideas or things that will make life easier doesn't solve the problem. There needs to be a seriousness involved.

My daughter, Angel, taught for the first time at church on her thirteenth birthday. I'll never forget the message: Matthew 7:7. She told us to A-S-K: *ask*, *seek*, and *knock*.

> "Keep asking, and it will be given to you; keep seeking, and you will find; keep knocking, and the door will be opened to you. For everyone who keeps asking receives; he who keeps seeking finds; and to him who keeps knocking, the door will be opened. Is there anyone here who, if his son asks him for a loaf

> of bread, will give him a stone? or if he asks for a fish, will give him a snake? So if you, even though you are bad, know how to give your children gifts that are good, how much more will your Father in heaven keep giving good things to those who keep asking him!" (Matthew 7:7–11 CJB)

Sometimes the goal of getting straight As might seem overwhelming, but staying focused and determined will make the goal attainable. Strong addictions may be challenging, but what good goal is not? The student who gets Fs may first move up to a D and gradually work up to an A. I am a believer that the Lord can instantly take away all uncleanliness. Yet I, in my limited understanding, can't assure that God handles all of His children the same. Whether a student goes from Fs straight to As or has to work their way up gradually isn't as important as the final goal. The important thing to remember is to keep at it. The Lord is a rewarder of those who *diligently* seek Him.

God's truth is to be applied in all areas of our lives. Often it can be easy for us to believe God can bring about change when we have small problems. We understand that He is able to help us with things that are easy fixes. Sometimes, when it comes to things like sickness and disease, we tend to forget that God really is God! By His power Jesus was raised to life. That same power lives in us if we have been born again.

It has been more and more difficult to ignore all the different ailments and syndromes in our world. It seems as if healthcare workers come up with a new name for a different ailment every day. Along with these ailments come drugs to cope with them. I find it very instructive that these "issues" were handled differently by Christ. When a person had a seizure, for example, Jesus commanded the demon to leave, and it went! Today, the "patient" is put on drugs and taught ways to "cope" with the "disorder."

Many believers have indeed prayed for their loved ones to be free from these types of bondages and often become discouraged when they see no change. The disciples also experienced this when they witnessed Jesus healing the boy with epilepsy. They could not understand why they were unable to cast the demon out of the boy themselves.

> And when they had come to the multitude, a man came to Him, kneeling down to Him and saying, "Lord, have mercy on my son,

for he is an epileptic and suffers severely; for he often falls into the fire and often into the water. So I brought him to Your disciples, but they could not cure him."

Then Jesus answered and said, "O faithless and perverse generation, how long shall I be with you? How long shall I bear with you? Bring him here to Me." And Jesus rebuked the demon, and it came out of him; and the child was cured from that very hour.

Then the disciples came to Jesus privately and said, "Why could we not cast it out?"

So Jesus said to them, "Because of your unbelief; for assuredly, I say to you, if you have faith as a mustard seed, you will say to this mountain, 'Move from here to there,' and it will move; and nothing will be impossible for you. However, this kind does not go out except by prayer and fasting." (Matthew 17:14–21 NKJV)

When we pray, we are told that we must believe that we will receive what we are asking for. We are even warned that praying without believing is double-minded, and the double-minded person will not receive anything from God. There are situations however, that call for more than just belief. Verse 21 in the quoted passage says that "this kind" does not go out of a person except by prayer and fasting. Certain things, like desiring all As, require more than just believing that you can do it. Sure, belief is the first and most important step. But our belief is proved by action! Salvation is the same. First, a person must believe that Jesus is the Son of God, that He died for our sin and rose to life again. But he also must be a witness or share his faith with someone as a testimony of his salvation. Likewise, prayer and fasting are a requirement when the stronghold over a loved one is this severe. It would be even better to have someone or a team of others who are willing to pray and fast with you. Remember, Christ said that if you believe, nothing will be impossible for you! We are not promised that things will be easy, yet we are reminded in His Word that "trouble produces endurance, endurance produces character, and character produces hope; and this hope does not let us down" (Romans 5:3–4 CJB). Endurance causes the runner to reach their goal!

I used to think that everyone should be free instantaneously. But after having children, I've begun to realize just how unique each individual is. Some people may have to be healed gradually, as doing so too quickly could cause damage or even death. Nature even teaches us that a mother weans her child gradually because doing so too abruptly could cause sickness in the mother and stress for the child. If, however, a child is allowed to continue to nurse well after an age that is appropriate, the child will lack necessary motor and social skills needed to reach milestones. Milk is for babies, not teenagers. Postponing weaning for too long could make for a severely handicapped life. We, as children of God, will have many milestones that should be reached and not avoided.

BELIEVING LIES

Many believers are comfortable living in bondage, simply because they have accepted the lie that it is OK to do so. Consider sexual sin: it puts not only those involved but others in their community in jeopardy as well, but no one dares to speak against it. It has even become socially acceptable to engage in sexual sins in the community of believers.

When half the church has a boyfriend or girlfriend, or sports inappropriate language or attire, no one says a word. If a guy misleads a young lady, she then, in her hurt and shame, acts out by provoking or tempting other men, looking for the love and validation she lost. Her clothing, or lack thereof, provides her the attention and reassurance that she always desired. She feels a false sense of empowerment as she saps the strength of even the strongest men around her. This woman's control over men is admired by other women, who also begin to act out. As the competition among the ladies increases, their morals and modesty decrease. More and more men lose their strength, respect, and honor to Jezebel-like women. The man's reputation is ruined, and he is destroyed (Proverbs 6:24–35 NIV). As a result, the men grow weaker, the women are exploited, and the children copy.

This filthy cycle continues because we are afraid to call evil, evil. When women are allowed to wear revealing or inappropriate clothing, or when a man is not confronted for being involved with someone who is not wearing his ring, we should expect trouble. There has been a twisting in the church amongst believers. We have sat quietly watching and allowing inappropriate behavior to continue. Believers are all too quick to quote scriptures that warn against judging others while completely ignoring 1 Corinthians 5 (NIV). This chapter instructs us not only to judge fellow believers but to kick them out of the church! This may seem harsh on the surface, but it is very necessary.

Verse 6 of this same chapter offers a warning in comparison to leaven. We can naturally understand that it only takes a little yeast to ferment a batch of dough, or as the world puts it, “One rotten apple will spoil the whole barrel.” Even when doing laundry, everyone knows that moldy, stinky, soiled clothes should not be folded and put into drawers with the clean. However, when it comes to spiritual things, we fail to correct sin when we see it. Spiritual housecleaning is necessary for the body of Christ to be healthy and whole. Allowing perversion to continue in the church only corrupts and sickens everyone, from the strong to the weak.

HIS CHILDREN

Over the years, I’ve talked to many Christians who make light of growing. I’ve heard excuses like “Well, God is just not done with me yet” or “Yeah, I’m still kinda disobedient in that area.” What father takes delight in a disobedient child?

Disobedience is rebellion, and rebellion is just as bad as the sin of witchcraft. If you think about it, it's pretty silly for us to call ourselves children of God yet make light of our disobedience. But not all who say that they are children of God are His children.

The Lord desires His children to grow and develop. They don't all grow up at the same time, but they do actually grow. We are running a race, and no one standing around should ever expect to win a prize. Jesus is our prize, and He has already won against Satan. Therefore, it would be reckless and evil of us to refuse progress. We are to press into the freedom that is ours. Why should we have to press if Christ has already won the battle? Well, I would humbly suppose that it's a lot like the doughnuts. The gift is out on the table, a free gift to anyone who asks. Only those who are truly hungry will go after it with fervor. The lazy and satisfied will say, "Thanks for the doughnut," but will ungratefully and slothfully lie around and wait for their parents to bring it to them. Saying that we want something is different from truly wanting it. My husband didn't just say that he wanted to marry me. He went out and bought a ring. He had to pay a price for the ring to prove that he was serious. He also had to book the church, pay the pastor for his services, and gather his groomsmen. What woman is there who would remain hoping for a promised marriage with no ring, no date, and no assurance? After some time, will she not want more than just his words?

James 2:26 (CJB) tells us that "just as the body without a spirit is dead, so too faith without actions is dead." How can we claim to have faith in God and in the power of God yet continue in a state of bondage? There may be a time of speaking those things that are not as though they were; for example, claiming, "I am no longer bound by the spirit of greed! I am the righteousness of Christ." Speaking into our lives this way can transform our thoughts about God's power that lives within us. But merely speaking this way is not enough. We then need to walk it out! For some this may mean to stop going to certain places or even severing relationships that would halt or prevent growth.

I told my husband that it seems like the Lord always leads me to speak a hard word or behave harshly to people. It's not very easy for me to do because I tend to be a little more passive by nature. But ultimately, I have a decision to make. Is my goal to please my Father, or frail man? If we choose to please the Lord in our decisions in life, we may end up offending many people. But it's better to offend man than to offend God, the Creator of man. So when moving forward, some people may have to be removed in order for you to grow and mature, but it is worth it.

LIKE FATHER, LIKE SON

Striving to be like the Father takes effort, it doesn't just come by chance. This is a touchy subject, but here it is anyhow! Who's yo' Daddy?!

> "Not everyone who says to me, 'Lord, Lord,' will enter the kingdom of heaven, but only the one who does the will of my Father who is in heaven. Many will say to me on that day, 'Lord, Lord, did we not prophesy in your name and in your name drive out demons and in your name perform many miracles?' Then I will tell them plainly, 'I never knew you. Away from me, you evildoers!' (Matthew 7:21–23 NIV)

Not everyone who says "Lord, Lord" will enter in. That scripture has a way of keeping me humble, especially the fact that it says *many*, and not few.

Many people hang their hat on being under grace and not under the law. Therefore, everything becomes permissible and OK with God because, after all, we are under grace. Jesus tells us plainly that only those that do the will of the Father will enter into the kingdom. Even Paul asks in Romans 6:

> Shall we go on sinning so that grace may increase? By no means! We are those who have died to sin; how can we live in it any longer? He even goes on to say, … we know that our old self was crucified with him so that the body ruled by sin might be done away with, that we should no longer be slaves to sin—because anyone who has died has been set free from sin. Now if we died with Christ, we believe that we will also live with him. For we know that since Christ was raised from the dead, he cannot die again; death no longer has mastery over him. The death he died, he died to sin once for all; but the life he lives, he lives to God. In the same way, count yourselves dead to sin but alive to God in Christ Jesus. Therefore do not let sin reign in your mortal

> body so that you obey its evil desires. Do not offer any part of yourself to sin as an instrument of wickedness, but rather offer yourselves to God as those who have been brought from death to life; and offer every part of yourself to him as an instrument of righteousness. For sin shall no longer be your master, because you are not under the law, but under grace. (Romans 6:1–2, 6–14 NIV)

Before we are saved, we are slaves to sin. We do things that do not please God because He is not yet our Father. However, we understand that everyone who is born has a father, and the same is true spiritually. We are children of either God or Satan. In the natural realm, we cannot choose who our father will be, but when it comes to our spiritual dad, we have a choice. And just as a son mimics the mannerisms, language, and actions of his father, our spirit-man mimics our spiritual father, whoever he may be. So how we talk is a clue to whom we follow, but even more so to how we live.

> When Jesus spoke again to the people, he said, "I am the light of the world. Whoever

follows me will never walk in darkness, but will have the light of life." …

So Jesus said, "When you have lifted up the Son of Man, then you will know that I am he and that I do nothing on my own but speak just what the Father has taught me. The one who sent me is with me; he has not left me alone, for I always do what pleases him." …

To the Jews who had believed him, Jesus said, "If you hold to my teaching, you are really my disciples. Then you will know the truth, and the truth will set you free." They answered him, "We are Abraham's descendants and have never been slaves of anyone. How can you say that we shall be set free?" Jesus replied, "Very truly I tell you, everyone who sins is a slave to sin. Now a slave has no permanent place in the family, but a son belongs to it forever. So if the Son sets you free, you will be free indeed." …

"Abraham is our father," they answered.

> "If you were Abraham's children," said Jesus, "then you would do what Abraham did. As it is, you are looking for a way to kill me, a man who has told you the truth that I heard from God. Abraham did not do such things. You are doing the works of your own father."
>
> "We are not illegitimate children," they protested. "The only Father we have is God himself."
>
> Jesus said to them, "If God were your Father, you would love me, for I have come here from God. I have not come on my own; God sent me. Why is my language not clear to you? Because you are unable to hear what I say. You belong to your father, the devil. (John 8:12, 28–29, 31–36, 39–43 NIV)

The fact that Jesus spoke only what He heard the Father say changes what could be just words to truth! Anyone can speak with boldness, but words have no substance if they are not God's words.

After Jesus told the religious crowd who their true father

was, they tried to stone Him. Wow! When reading accounts like this, we should ask the Lord to allow us to remain humble and not fall into the category of stoning His messengers. We should never become too proud to be corrected. With wisdom comes humility. Are you humble enough to be told that you are wrong? I hope so. Because it is when we have been corrected that we can be groomed and nurtured by the Father.

> My son, do not despise the Lord's discipline,
> and do not resent his rebuke,
> because the Lord disciplines those he loves,
> as a father the son he delights in. (Proverbs 3:11–12 NIV)

BEING WAY TOO COMFORTABLE

The children of Israel had been living in Egypt for four hundred years. They ate, slept, and lived in the land of Goshen. As a result, they became accustomed to the cuisine there. After God had rescued the Israelites with His mighty hand, the children of Israel began to complain about their new way of eating. While they were in the wilderness, the

Lord rained down manna. The Israelites were fed the food of angels and were given all that they needed to thrive.

> And the mixed multitude among them [the rabble who followed Israel from Egypt] began to lust greatly [for familiar and dainty food], and the Israelites wept again and said, Who will give us meat to eat? We remember the fish we ate freely in Egypt and without cost, the cucumbers, melons, leeks, onions, and garlic. But now our soul (our strength) is dried up; there is nothing at all [in the way of food] to be seen but this manna. (Numbers 11:4–6 AMPC)

After a while, they began to get tired of the monotonous taste. They started to complain about the food that rained down from heaven to feed them! They thought back on the food they had in Egypt. However, it is probably more important to take note of what is stated before their complaints. The mixed multitude among them, or riffraff in another translation, began to lust or crave for their old familiar food. Their cravings began to influence the children of Israel. Who knows—the Israelites may have complained with or without the influence of the bystanders. Yet people are influenced by the company they keep: "Do not be misled: Bad company corrupts good character" (1 Corinthians 15:33 NIV).

If freedom from a particular bondage is sought, in most if not all cases, old ties need to be severed. Sometimes it is an old friend or just an old way of thinking that needs to be removed from our lives. If the ties that are to be cut are indeed people, then so be it! So many people are afraid to leave old friendships for fear of offending loved ones or gaining a bad reputation. But these things are of little importance in light of living life to the fullest! Scripture tells us that

> He who walks with wise men will be wise,
> But the companion of fools will be destroyed.
> (Proverbs 13:20 NKJV)

Most of us find our comfort in the relationships we keep. We would not welcome the thought of ending a close relationship that has supplied us with intimacy and security. We understand that without certain people around us, we may feel uneasy. But if the relationship is one that is pulling us into sin and bondage, it needs to end. Life is precious, and we should acknowledge that it is a gift from God. The people we are around will affect the life that we are given. While it is important for us to protect our close relationships, I believe it is much more important to be good stewards of the gift we have been entrusted with. Sometimes keeping away from distracting relationships not only protects us but others as well. God is eternal, as is our relationship with Him. It is much more important to protect healthy relationships, even at the expense of terminating bad ones.

PRIDE

It seems that all believers would desire freedom from the grip of Satan. However, so many remain bound! Sometimes believers remain in bondage due to pride. Humility acknowledges that there is a problem with sin that needs to be addressed.

Unfortunately, to humble oneself is not part of the plan for most. When we previously discussed the bondage in the way that we think, I'm certain that some were heavily offended. After all, to suggest that your thinking could be corrupt not only offends the thinker but calls into account the very soul of a man. If our way of thinking is not in line with the Word of

God, it has an alignment with something else. It is important for us to take on the mind of Christ.

> Do nothing out of selfish ambition or vain conceit. Rather, in humility value others above yourselves, not looking to your own interests but each of you to the interests of the others.
>
> In your relationships with one another, have the same mindset as Christ Jesus:
>
> Who, being in very nature God,
> did not consider equality with God something to be used to his own advantage;
> rather, he made himself nothing
> by taking the very nature of a servant,
> being made in human likeness.
> And being found in appearance as a man,
> he humbled himself
> by becoming obedient to death—
> even death on a cross!

> Therefore God exalted him to the highest place
>
> and gave him the name that is above every name,
>
> that at the name of Jesus every knee should bow,
>
> in heaven and on earth and under the earth. (Philippians 2:3–10 NIV)

Christ, we are told, humbled Himself even to the death of His flesh. After the humiliation of His physical death, God highly exalted Him. Therefore, at the very name of Jesus, every knee, both in heaven and on earth, must bow before Him. Before we are given Christ's example, we are instructed in verse 3 above to humble ourselves and to esteem others. However, the world, through the lies of our enemy that is constantly twisting the Word of God, tells us to have self-esteem. Self-esteem is the very thing that we are constantly warned against.

It was self-esteem that caused the children of Israel to go into captivity. Self-esteem persuaded the religious rulers in Jesus's time to desire His death and defeat. It was also self-esteem that got Satan thrown out of the presence of God! Not much has changed; even today, people are still worshippers of self. Self-esteem has produced a narcissistic breed of zombies that live and breathe off self-promotion. The average cell phone holds pages upon pages of selfies. Social media is drowned by posts of the day-to-day thoughts and activities that people think others want to hear about and see them do. It's no wonder things like drugs and sex are abused. If my concern is esteeming myself, I do what pleases me, not you or God! This way of thinking allows an adulterer to cheat on their spouse and even excuse their own behavior with complaints about the one they promised to be faithful to.

In my humble opinion, I believe that all of us at some point in our lives have had a problem with pride. Whether the result was murder, drugs, or self-esteem, pride is still pride. Before you boast of never having murdered or fornicated, consider what Jesus said.

> "You have heard that our fathers were told, 'Do not murder,' and that anyone who commits murder will be subject to judgment. But I tell you that anyone who nurses anger against his brother will be subject to

> judgment; that whoever calls his brother, 'You good-for-nothing!' will be brought before the Sanhedrin; that whoever says, 'Fool!' incurs the penalty of burning in the fire of Gei-Hinnom! [hellfire] …
>
> "You have heard that our fathers were told, 'Do not commit adultery.' But I tell you that a man who even looks at a woman with the purpose of lusting after her has already committed adultery with her in his heart." (Matthew 5:21–22, 27–28 CJB)

The teachings of Jesus rid us of our boasting. It is very important that we keep ourselves humble and teachable. It is deceptive for us to look on the sins of others with contempt and give a pass to our own gossip, slander, and boasts.

I think everyone knows someone who loves mirrors. Every time they walk past one, they just have to stop in admiration. I've heard someone say, "I've never met a mirror that I didn't like." Unfortunately, mirrors only give a reflection of the outward appearance. When we examine ourselves, it is important for us to look at the inner man. Mirrors, in a sense, tell a lie. They assure the narcissist that their eyes are clear and bright, their nose is clean, and their teeth are white and without spots! The lover of self never looks any deeper than the surface. When we examine ourselves, we are to look much deeper. If our eyes truly are a mirror to the soul, what have we been exposing our eyes to? Whose business have we been sticking our noses in? Have we been crucifying the Lord's children with the sword we call our tongue?

Many of us have walked around with dirty hands, doing damage by destroying others instead of building them up. It's time to put down the surface mirrors and pick up the true ones. When we examine ourselves, it is vital that we do so honestly. Our souls depend on it! Pride is in the heart of almost every person. We are too quick to see the shortcomings of everyone else. But we must be willing to recognize our own lusts, adulteries, witchcrafts, fornications, lies, boasts, manipulations, murders, robberies, backbiting, and prideful thoughts. Pride is the enemy of God. If we truly desire freedom from bondage, pride must go, and humility must rule in our hearts.

Humbling ourselves daily is essential to both becoming and remaining free!

FEAR

Most of us associate fear with negative things. But it just depends on what is feared. We all should fear *something*, but it's the something that determines whether or not our fear is good or bad.

> The fear of *Adonai* is the beginning of wisdom,
> and knowledge of holy ones is understanding.
> (Proverbs 9:10 CJB)

We are instructed throughout the Word to fear God. This verse from Proverbs tells us that fear is the beginning of wisdom—the beginning, meaning the very first and principal thing.

In his *Exposition of the Entire Bible*, the eighteenth-century Calvinist theologian John Gill states,

> fear is an awe and reverence of the divine Being, joined with love to him, trust in him, and a desire to serve and worship him in a right manner; no sooner is a man converted, but presently there is in him a fear of offending

> God, from a principle of love to him; for not a slavish but a filial fear is here intended.

The beginning of wisdom is the fear, reverence, adoration, worship, and desire of or for God.

All of us, even those who claim to be atheists, fear God or a god. The wisdom, or lack thereof, lies in whomever or whatever that God or god is. If indeed the fear of the Lord is the beginning of wisdom, and knowledge of the holy ones is understanding, what does its opposite look like?

> If you are wise, your wisdom helps you;
> but if you scoff, you bear the consequences alone. (Proverbs 9:12 CJB)

Those who are void of wisdom don't fear God. If we are not careful to fear the Lord, we will surely fear our enemy and live our lives destined for destruction. Wisdom and foolishness are opposites, and no one can possess wisdom without the fear of God.

> The foolish woman is coarse;
> she doesn't think, and she doesn't know a thing.
> She sits at the door of her house

> or on a seat at the heights of the city,
> calling to those who pass by,
> to those going straight along their ways,
> "Whoever is unsure of himself, turn in here!"
> To someone weak-willed she says,
> "Stolen water is sweet;
> food eaten in secret is pleasant."
> But he doesn't realize
> that the dead are there,
> and that those who accept her invitation
> are in the depths of Sh'ol. (Proverbs 9:13–18 CJB)

The fear of God keeps us from going down the wrong street in the first place—whatever we revere, we keep ever before us. We meditate and dwell on the things we are passionate about. When our chief and principal thought is the Lord, there is little or no room for foolish thinking and activities. God grows and grooms us with His loving and nurturing hands. If we love and fear Him, He grants us the wisdom needed for our spiritual growth and development. Fearing God over anyone or anything else is crucial to gaining and retaining wisdom, knowledge, and understanding.

FOOLISHNESS

As previously stated, the opposite of wisdom is foolishness. Sometimes all we know is foolishness. There are things that we, in our limited understanding, misunderstand. For as long as we are on this earth, we will have some lack of understanding of things.

> What we see now is like a dim image in a mirror; then we shall see face-to-face. What I know now is only partial; then it will be complete—as complete as God's knowledge of me. (1 Corinthians 13:12 GNT)

We look forward to the time in which we will see things more clearly. But while we are here occupying our time on earth, we press forward to more growth.

> Foolishness is bound up in
> The heart of a child;
> The rod of correction will
> drive it far from him. (Proverbs 22:15 NKJV)

It's not until we have received discipline that we begin to learn what is acceptable and unacceptable. Although it is true that we will retain a degree of immaturity to some degree while here on earth, this understanding should never be an excuse to remain that way. Being born foolish isn't an excuse for remaining prisoners of sin. As we gain more understanding, freedom becomes easier to access.

I grew up in a single-parent home with three brothers. We were poor, and so were most of the families in our neighborhood. Poverty was all we knew; it was our way of life. Some nights were cold, and sometimes we were hungry. And although I was the only girl, I didn't escape hand-me-downs. My cousin's old clothes were my prized inheritance. My brothers and I don't resent being poor; in fact, I believe that it was a blessing. Our hardships caused us to be grateful in all things. My brothers are all married and make very thoughtful and mature financial decisions that are a blessing to their families. I'm very proud of their maturity and ability to see beyond what they had seen in life.

It was, however, a little harder for me to break free from the curse of poverty. My limited thinking of using money just to pay bills and not investing had caused me to remain limited to "just enough." My husband is adventurous and unlimited! His willingness to take risks to grow our money was, in my fearful opinion, both foolish and reckless.

If either of these two ways of thinking goes unchecked, poverty is assured. I know that the Lord has specifically joined us in matrimony to break the bonds of poverty! Wisdom is balanced decision-making that breaks us away from our old ways of thinking. Trusting the Lord often translates to women through trusting our husbands. For me, this didn't come easy. But realizing that God is in control and speaks to my husband as well as He does to me has changed my love and respect for each of his decisions. My husband, without my prodding, now actually seeks my advice before making most decisions. Thus each hand washes the other, and instead of seeing only our own point of view, we are able to make better decisions that benefit our family as well as others.

Poverty is a disease that has a cure. The antidote is found in the Word of God. Who would remain sick, knowing where to find the cure? I hope you won't. The Lord says that if we seek Him, we will find Him. As Angel so simply put it, A-S-K!

4

CHOOSING FREEDOM

Even when a book is guided by God, its wisdom and insight can go to waste if it is neglected by the reader. We have been given a great and terrible gift, the gift of a free will. God, our loving and nurturing Father, did not create robots or zombies that are forced to love and worship Him. Instead, He formed a man. He created him to have the freedom to choose love or defiance, obedience or rebellion, freedom or bondage, life or death. After giving man all the options, God, in His great love toward us, instructs us to "choose life." Like a loving parent, the child is provided with the answers for success in life. But the father cannot live life for his son; he must allow the boy to make his own decisions.

Just as parents truly want the best for their children, the Father wants the best for us. Through His Word, He provides us with His holy teachings full of all the wisdom and knowledge needed to live holy lives and to have good success. Yet very few of us spend the time to study and search out His precepts. We know that His wisdom is very deep and is hidden from mankind, yet we are told that He desires to be sought after. It's strange how often we will search out things that captivate and intrigue us but will make excuses for not studying the very Word of God. It amazes me that in

His glorious splendor, He considers us enough to speak to us through His Word. He gives us good gifts—even His own Son to die in our place! As if that wasn't enough, He gifted us with His very Spirit after Jesus was lifted into heaven. His Holy Spirit has taken up residence in the heart of fallen man when we accept it from the Father.

It is important for us to realize that there are two things working within us. Our flesh is in direct opposition to the Spirit of God dwelling within. Who will be the strongest? Aha! That's the big question. The answer changes from person to person. Whichever we feed the most, whether the flesh or the Spirit, will eventually grow the strongest.

> Don't delude yourselves: no one makes a fool of God! A person reaps what he sows. Those who keep sowing in the field of their old nature, in order to meet its demands, will eventually reap ruin; but those who keep sowing in the field of the Spirit will reap from the Spirit, everlasting life. So let us not grow weary of doing what is good; for if we don't give up, we will in due time reap the harvest. (Galatians 6:7–9 CJB)

God is gracious. He gives us the answers to the tests in life. He then leaves it to us to study and prepare. Just as we feed the body food that fuels it to move, think, and live, we need to feed the Spirit with the Word of God. If we starve the Holy Spirit, and spend our time practicing and making a habit of things that are not holy, the flesh will grow, making those strongholds harder to crucify. This was very evident in my struggle with sexual purity. It is important for us to gain spiritual muscle if we truly desire freedom. After all, no one in their right mind sits around feeding on chips and pop while claiming they want to be cut and defined with bulging muscles. Would you believe them? Of course not!

> Each tree is recognized by its own fruit—figs aren't picked from thorn bushes, nor grapes from a briar patch. (Luke 6:44 CJB)

We are warned again and again in scripture to beware of the wolves in sheep's clothing. Jesus spoke so often not just to the lost but also to the religious leaders. When He was hungry, he saw a fig tree from afar and expected to eat its fruit. But as He approached, He was disappointed to find only leaves and no fruit. The leaves remind me of our claim of salvation and righteous walk with Christ. I think of the leaves as the words we speak: "I'm saved, sanctified, and filled with the Holy Ghost!" Yet when Jesus went to eat the fruit of this tree, there was none! It's just like the lazy one we talked about, sitting around eating junk food claiming to want to be fit. Jesus expected fruit but found none. Forget about the sinner or religious leaders for a moment, and entertain the idea that this may have been written for us—yep, for you and me! The story concludes with Jesus cursing the fig tree (Mark 11:12 –14 NIV).

If I were one of the characters in this story, the last one I'd want to be is the fig tree. The fig tree looked as if it had something to offer the Lord. It appears pretty, lush, vibrant, and full of nourishment. Yet upon closer examination, it was not even in season and was unfruitful! How disappointed the Lord must have been.

My Abba

Here I stand in Awe and Reverence of Your Holiness.
It is Your presence that I am unable to resist.
Guard, Lord, my fickle heart and soul
From the dread and fear of stress and overload.

Help me to remain steadfast and fixed upon Thee,
ABBA; let nothing come between You and me.
Be my only passion, my One true desire.
It is Your perfect love from which I shall never retire.

Let nothing other than You capture my heart and attention.
I want none other, only Your love and affection.
Teach me Your precepts as I meditate on Your Perfect Word;
Take away all evil with the sharpness of Your Sword.

Reform this stubborn lump of clay
And fashion me in Your Perfect way.
You, the Lover of my soul, make me anew,
For without You guiding my life, I haven't a clue.

For You know all things; nothing is hidden from Thee.
It is Your Hand that shields the fiery darts of my enemy.
Thank You for breaking my chains and
granting freedom from oppression.
It is only You, my ABBA—You hold my absolute obsession!

Your beloved

CRYSTAL BOSWELL

WALKING IN FREEDOM

Jesus asked the woman who was being accused and sentenced to death, "Woman, where are those accusers of yours?" When there was no one left to accuse her, Jesus told her, "Neither do I condemn you." He let her go free and told her to leave her life of sin (John 8:3–11 NKJV).

I've heard people talk about this story most of my life. I've heard people explain it in terms of the people casting judgment on the adulteress woman, and Jesus pardoning her sin. But it wasn't until I began to study it myself that I found out about Jesus's command to the woman. He didn't just let her off the hook without any rules or instructions. No, He instructed her to leave her life of sin. How can so many people ignore such vital information?

I'd like to end our conversation by instructing you, my beloved brothers and sisters, to leave a life of sin. With the power of His Word, I say, "Go and sin no more!"

In Jesus name, amen.

Printed in the United States
by Baker & Taylor Publisher Services